HOW T...

A practical guide to the
Spiritual life

David Torkington

McCrimmons
Great Wakering Essex England

To Bobbie
Without whom this book
could never have been written

"To say your work is your prayer or your life is your
prayer is not only meaningless, but quite misleading.
It is undoubtedly the ideal, but such an ideal will never be
realised, outside the monastic way of life,
without giving daily time to personal prayer".

Cardinal Basil Hume

First published in the United Kingdom in 2002 by
McCrimmon Publishing Co. Ltd.
10-12 High Street, Great Wakering, Essex SS3 0EQ
Email: mccrimmons@dial.pipex.com
Website: www.mccrimmons.com

© 2002 David Torkington

ISBN 0 85597 638 1

British Library Cataloguing in Publication Data.
A catalogue record for this book is available from the British Library.

Cover design by Alan Hencher
Page layout by Nick Snode

Typeset in 10/14 ITC Symbol Medium
Printed and bound by Black Bear Press Ltd., Cambridge, England

Contents

Foreword

WE CAN SO EASILY READ about prayer, about love, about Christian service and in the emotional happiness of our reading come to think that we are actually doing what we are only feeling. Fortunately no one is more aware of this danger than David Torkington. He is passionately committed to stripping from the reader those veils of illusion that allow what is said to be enjoyed in theory only.

His subtitle is 'A practical guide to the Spiritual life' and that is precisely what he earnestly sets himself to provide. There are no hideaways here, no excuses, but no alarming demands either. Torkington seeks only to show us the truth, that truth that sets us free and convinces us that the yoke of Jesus is easy and his burden light. All we need is to understand and to choose.

This book offers us the help we need to understand and then the choice is ours.

Sr Wendy Beckett

Introduction

Although people go on crying out for solutions they become angry when they are told that the restoration of society must come from within and not from without.

Schumacher – 'Small is beautiful'

THE EVIL THAT WE READ ABOUT daily in our newspapers or see on our television screens is but the outward projection of the evil that is firstly conceived and spawned within the human heart and mind. That's why, when she was asked how one could combat the woes of the world, St Catherine of Siena said, "The trouble with the world is me."

It's all too easy to blame God or ask why He doesn't prevent evil when it tears our lives apart or the lives of the innocent for whom we can do nothing but offer sympathy. But the truth of the matter is that God is at all times poised to possess anyone who is open to receive the love that only He can give. It is this love that brings the profound inner peace that Jesus promised on the night before He died, so that it can be shared with the world that will always be at war without it. However, love cannot be forced on anyone who does not freely choose to receive it. If we are eaten up with hatred or jealousy, or possessed by pride or prejudice it is we, not God, who are responsible for destroying the peace and harmony that He wants to bring to the world through us.

St Catherine of Siena saw so clearly what she should do to enable God to make her into the greatest politician for peace in her time. She went into the 'inner room' to give prolonged periods of time to prayer to enable the love of God to purify her of all the evil that could prevent her receiving the peace that she was able to share with the world around her.

The message is so simple that it needs the simplicity of the child to see what cynics can only scoff at. We are not helpless, we can do something to combat the evil that we see in the world around us, if we are only prepared to go like St Catherine into the 'inner room'. It is only here that we can seriously turn to the only One who can first bring to us what He would bring to the world that He now chooses to serve through us.

This little book has been written for those who are ready to accept this truth to help them to enable God to bring about in them what He wants to bring about in all. It is only in this way that His Kingdom, or His rule of love may reign where bitterness and hatred ruled before.

1   Transforming love

> *There is only one way to perfection*
> *and that is to pray.*
> *If anyone points in another direction*
> *then they are deceiving you.*

St Teresa of Avila

I WAS ONLY NINE YEARS OLD when I learned my first lesson in philosophy thanks to the conjurer at my friend's birthday party. I was chosen to examine the inside of his top hat to prove that there was nothing in it. Then he draped everything in sight with silk handkerchiefs, flags and bouquets of flowers. When I told my father what I'd seen he said he couldn't possibly have taken something out of nothing. If there was nothing in the hat then nothing could have come out of it. There was either something hidden inside it that I hadn't seen, or something hidden up the conjurer's sleeve. My father wasn't a spoilsport, he was just trying to teach me something that I've never forgotten. Something cannot come from nothing. The 'Big Bang' then, or whatever else brought the Universe into being, cannot have been preceded by nothing. It must have been preceded by something.

No matter how sophisticated it might be, 'some thing' couldn't produce the highest form of energy which is love. Whatever was responsible for creation therefore, must be 'someone'. Only a person can produce love. Love can no more come from 'some thing' than something can come from nothing!

That's why the Gospel states quite clearly that God, in whom and by whom all things were created, is love. That's what He was, that's what He is, and that's what He does. So I suppose it would be more accurate to say that God is not so much love, but loving. The Gospel is the story of how this loving progressively penetrated the human nature of Jesus Christ. It was the tangible experience of being loved by God that was the source of His inner security and strength. It made Him the most perfect and the most loveable person to have walked on this earth. His prime purpose in life was to tell people where the love that animated Him comes from and then to show them how to receive and experience it for themselves, transforming them into ever more perfect human beings. Prayer is the word used to describe how a person freely chooses to turn towards God to receive and then to assimilate this love until it unites us with Him. This is the only way that the Gospel precept can be observed, to be perfect, as God is perfect.

2 The little back shop

We should keep for ourselves a little back shop, all our own, untouched by others, in which we establish our true freedom and chief place of seclusion and solitude.

Montaigne

TRUE FREEDOM doesn't mean to be free from, but to be free for the most important thing in our lives, which is to love and to experience being loved. Jesus wanted to receive and experience His Father's love more than anything else. Then He wanted to return it and share what He had received with others. This meant that He had to structure His life in such a way that He could continually have access to the love that would give Him, in ever fuller measure, what He wanted to share with others. That's why He regularly went to the temple and to the synagogue with His disciples, and that's why He often went alone for more prolonged personal prayer into lonely places, to the inner room, to the mountainside and into the garden 'where it was His custom to pray'. However in addition to all this He needed regular daily personal prayer as we do.

It was the custom of orthodox Jews at that period to pray at prescribed times of the day as Muslims do today. Jesus would have done the same and taught His followers to do likewise. Furthermore He taught them how to do it in such a manner that they would avoid the ostentatious way many of the Pharisees prayed in public to draw attention to themselves. When you pray, he insisted, "go to your private room and, when you have shut your door in that secret place, your father who sees all that is done in secret will reward you." When lifestyles and work-patterns changed in subsequent centuries Christians no longer found it possible to stick to the prescribed times that Jesus would have used with His disciples, so the practice of morning and evening prayer began to take their place. Sadly in recent years they seem to be disappearing, like grace before and after meals, which are all too often eaten on a tray in front of the 'telly'.

It's time to start again by setting up that little back shop so that we can retire into it every morning and evening to find there the inner freedom to receive and experience the self-same love that inspired Jesus and transformed everything He did. This Love will change us like nothing else on earth, making us more loveable and enabling us to love those we already love more deeply and even those we've never loved before.

3 The school for love

You must repent and then you will receive the gift of the Holy Spirit.

St Peter

HUMAN BEINGS are made of body and spirit, so when they love their loving is both spiritual and physical at one and the same time. However God has no body, so when He loves, He loves with His Spirit alone. As a mark of reverence therefore, His love has traditionally been called 'The Holy Spirit'.

The Spiritual life is the expression used to describe a new way of life, organised by someone who wants to start turning towards God regularly, in order to receive His love or His Holy Spirit. First and foremost this means building a prayer life that leads through meditation to contemplation where a person is more open to receiving God's love than ever before. However to begin with it is necessary to set aside quality space and time each day as Jesus Himself did in order to practise turning to God regularly.

Most people give up before they've started because they think that distractions make prayer impossible. The truth is they would never learn to pray without them. Each time they turn away from a distraction to turn back to God they perform an act of selflessness. If they repeatedly perform acts of selflessness in this way a habit of selflessness is gradually formed. This enables them to be open to receive the love of God for ever longer periods of time. That's why prayer is often called 'a school of divine love'. It is the place where loving is learnt by those who are prepared to go on giving day after day though it might seem, at least to begin with, that they receive nothing in return. The word repentance is used in the scriptures to describe the act of turning back to God despite the distractions that try to turn our attention elsewhere. That's why Jesus continually called people to repent so that they could be continually open to receive the self-same love that He received.

Prayer then is a school that specialises in teaching the selflessness that enables a person to love God in such a way that His love can be received in return. The more selflessness is learnt in this way then the more a person is able to experience the love that they receive, making them more and more loveable not only to God but also to everybody else.

4   Pray, don't babble

When you pray don't babble as pagans do, for they think by using many words they will make themselves heard.

Jesus Christ (Matthew 6:7)

IF WE'VE NEVER SERIOUSLY PRAYED to God before, except when we wanted something out of Him, it's understandably difficult to get started. Inevitably our first attempts at entering into some sort of 'conversation' with Him can seem to be rather cold and even stereotyped to begin with and more like a monologue than a dialogue. However, that will all change in time if we are prepared to keep at it. One of our main problems is that we get lost for words and before we know what has happened we find our minds are deluged with a thousand and one distractions.

That's why it's important to aim at being as simple and straightforward as possible in the words we use. Remember what Jesus taught – namely, that God is our Father, even our loving Dad. That's why he told us to call Him Abba, so there's no need to speak to Him in fancy phrases or highfalutin language. "O God we beseech thee in thy infinite goodness, vouchsafe to thy humble servant…" – you know the sort of thing I mean. Remember Jesus criticised the Pharisees severely for doing this. We ought to use our own words whenever possible.

Naturally this might be difficult to begin with. If it is we can always start by using someone else's words, their prayers, gradually transposing them into our own. However, it's important never to lose sight of the ideal, which is to get rid of them as soon as possible, as soon as we are able to use our own words.

One thing is absolutely necessary from the start and that is to be completely honest with God. Nothing short of total frankness is called for when we start to pray. Don't forget that God knows us through and through even before we open our mouths. We might be able to 'soft-soap' others, but we can't fool God, so why try. If you feel like a dehydrated prune you should say so, if you'd rather be sitting in front of the telly, admit it, and if you'd sooner be reading the paper or a fast moving thriller, why pretend you wouldn't.

Words aren't so difficult to find in prayer if we only try to speak simply and honestly and are prepared to admit exactly how we feel from the word go.

5   The 'Parousia'

The Mass should so form us that the whole of our lives becomes the Mass, the place where we continually offer ourselves through Christ to the Father.

Karl Rahner

ALTHOUGH IN THE END it's best to use our own words, in the beginning we can't do better than by using the words of someone who is more experienced than ourselves. Who better than Jesus Himself and the prayer He taught us? We should always begin our daily prayer with His, then in our own words try to mould ourselves into His prayer in its most perfect expression at the Last Supper. Here the most perfect prayer and the most perfect action of the most perfect person became as one. It is repeated for all time in the Eucharist for us to share in it. Although we can't always be physically present to share in the Sacred Mysteries each day we can share in them spiritually by moulding our daily prayer as perfectly as we can into His.

Here's a memory jog that I use to do just this – try it – it might be of help to you. Take the Greek word '*Parousia*', used to describe the arrival of a King. It was used when the scriptures were translated into Greek to describe the threefold coming of Christ. His first coming in history, His final coming in majesty and, between the two, His continual coming in mystery. St Peter sees the time between the first coming in history and the final coming in majesty as a time for repentance or a time for repeatedly turning to receive the Christ who continually comes to us in mystery through love. That's why prayer is so important. It is the place where we continually turn to receive Him into our lives and into our prayer so that we may be perfectly fitted into His. I use each letter of the Greek word '*Parousia*' to remind me of eight simple Latin words.

Each of these is a reminder of eight essential ingredients of prayer, as embodied in the Mass that should characterise our daily prayer. The words are – **Professio** (profession), **Adoratio**, (adoration), **Reconciliatio** (reconciliation), **Offerta** (offering), **Unio** (union), **Silentio** (silence), **Intercessio** (intercession), and **Actio** (action). Each of these helps to fit us into the most perfect prayer of Christ that embodies all that He has done, is doing and will continue to do, so that 'we may have life and have it in ever greater abundance'.

6   A profession of faith

Professio   (profession)

> *'Twas much that God became like Man before but that man should be made like God much more.*

John Donne

ALWAYS BEGIN PRAYER with a profession of faith. I don't mean by reciting some traditional formula of faith or even professing belief in every article of the creed or in every dogma that the Church teaches. There is a time and place for that, however this is the time for something else. Our faith, you see, is not firstly a belief in a body of truths but in a body full of love that was filled to overflowing on the first Easter Day.

Ever since the first Pentecost Day God's love has been pouring out of Jesus and into all who freely choose to receive it, to draw them into the fullness of life that is fully embodied in His risen body, sometimes called His Mystical Body. It is here alone that we are all destined 'to live and move and have our being' and experience something of the ecstatic bliss that Jesus experiences now and to all eternity.

That's one more reason why the fish became a symbol of a Christian in the early Church. They came to see and understand that the love of God was for them what the sea is for the fish, the living environment outside of which they could not exist. St Augustine takes this analogy one step further, substituting a living sponge for the fish to show that we are not only surrounded at all times by the love of God but are penetrated through and through by His all pervading presence. This loving presence is the supernatural environment in which we can grow, becoming ever more perfect Christ-like human beings.

Although this is the profound truth in which we express our faith at the beginning of prayer we may rarely experience anything, at least to begin with. Much more often than not we have to accept in faith what Christ continually experiences and what we'd like to experience one day for ourselves. Nevertheless this is the time to make a profound act of faith in this all-pervading presence of God's love. It's time to pray too that it will become more and more real to us, not just while we are at prayer, but throughout the forthcoming day and every day.

7   Adoration, praise and thanksgiving

Adoratio (adoration)

To adore means to lose oneself in the unfathomable, to plunge into the inexhaustible, to find peace in the incorruptible, to be absorbed into the immeasurable, and to give one's deepest to that whose depth has no end.

Teilhard de Chardin

THE REALISATION THAT THE 'All Holy and Utterly Other' has chosen to draw us into His own life should bring us physically, or at least metaphorically, to our knees in adoration. That's why the letter '*A*' should remind us to spend a few moments in quiet *Adoration*. This should naturally overflow into giving praise, glory, and thanksgiving to the One who, though He infinitely transcends us, has chosen to make His home in the very depth of our being – "make your home in me and I will make my home in you".

If words fail, to begin, with then express your adoration in someone else's words. Take your favourite prayer or hymn of praise, and adoration and give glory to God in those words. Take the 'Gloria' from the liturgy, for instance, and recite it slowly and prayerfully. Gradually you'll find you are taken out of yourself, out of your world and into God's world. Then you'll discover that the further you enter into His world the more you'll forget yourself and the world where you only lived for yourself. It is in this profound prayer that you will be raised beyond yourself if only for brief moments, where your prayer life will have reached higher peaks than ever before. Then you'll come alive, more alive than ever before, if only for a short time, in the world where you want to be for all time.

When the full impact of all that God has done for us begins to register on your inmost being it's time to give Him thanks over and over again for what He continually gives to us. We are all too ready to ask but sadly all too slow to thank God, not just for what He has done for us personally, but for His goodness, His beauty, and His loving kindness. We should also remember to thank Him for His inner glory reflected in creation and most of all, for the Masterpiece of creation whom He has sent to inhabit us through the Holy Spirit.

8   Reconciliation

Reconciliatio   (reconciliation)

When you come to prayer inspect your heart, so as to send your prayer pure to God, and carefully examine whether there is any obstacle to this.

Abbot Macarius the Egyptian

THE THANKS THAT GOD really wants to receive more than anything else cannot be given in words alone. You see He wants us to do all that is within our power to enable Him to strip away all and everything in our lives that prevents us from being totally reconciled to Him. Only then will He be able to possess us as fully as He would wish. That's why the next letter in the memory-jog is '*R*' for '*Reconciliation*'. It is a reminder to pause for a few moments to review our lives since we last prayed. It's time to ask God to show us everything we have done or failed to do that has kept Him out. It is this that prevents Him from making His home within us as He promised on the night before He died. Then our prayer will rise from a pure and contrite heart.

I don't think it's healthy to encourage people to become morbidly introspective, but it is necessary to keep a close eye on the way we treat others and endeavour to live out the standards of Christian behaviour in our daily lives. That's why from the earliest times the practice of examining one's conscience grew rapidly, first amongst the Desert Fathers and then amongst those who were influenced by their spirituality.

Then it's time to make an 'Act of Contrition' for how we have failed in the past. A formal act of contrition could be used, but a sincere expression of personal sorrow, in our own words, would be better still. Then we could make what has traditionally been called 'a firm purpose of amendment'. If we don't intend to try better next time round it's ten to one that there was something seriously wrong with the sorrow that we expressed a few moments before.

Finally, on the basis of the review of life that has just been made, we should be a little more aware of the moral stumbling blocks that usually trip us up. Now, therefore, is the time to try and forestall them. If there is a lazy streak in us, or if we have a hot temper, or are prone to making 'smart alec' remarks at other peoples' expense, now is the time to take the necessary steps to avoid falling into these same faults in the forthcoming day. It's time to ask for God's help too to do what we won't be able to do without it.

9 The morning offering

Offerta (offering)

Christ does not offer alone, His people are joined to Him and offer with Him and through Him. Indeed they are absorbed into Him and form one body with Him by the Holy Spirit who lives in all.

Joseph Jungmann

GOD'S PLAN IS NOT JUST THAT we should be drawn up in Christ's life but be taken up into his action. So the next letter, '*O*', reminds us to join with Christ in '*Offering*' ourselves to our common Father. Despite all the offerings made in the past Christ made it clear to His followers that the only offering that God really wants in the future is the offering of ourselves. That's why we are all called to become priests because only we can offer ourselves, no one else can do it for us. That's why the early Christians were so aware of their priesthood. However only He can make that offering effective, because it's made through His.

Moreover, that's why they went to exercise it with others on the first day of the week, or Sunday as it came to be called. Then they would return to their own homes and to their own lives to use the help and strength that they had received, to offer every moment of every day to God as Christ Himself had done. Then, when they returned the following week, they would offer up all these sacrifices that they had made, to receive from God in return far more than they had given. In this way they would be caught up in an endless cycle of giving and receiving that would fit them ever more fully into the mystery of Christ.

The early Christians used to remind themselves each morning of how they could exercise their priesthood in the forthcoming day by offering all and everything they proposed to do through Christ's sacrifice to the Father. In later years this daily reminder evolved into what came to be called 'The Morning Offering'. It was this prayer that my mother taught me many years ago to remind me before each day began how I could become as she put it 'a little priest', turning ordinary commonplace things into something precious, as Rumplestiltskin turned straw into gold.

It was she then who first taught me about the priesthood to which we are all called in Christ, and how to put it into practice each day. She taught me, most of all by her own example, how the whole of life could become the Mass, the place where we continually offer ourselves through Christ to the Father through all we say and do.

10   Mystical union

Unio (union)

> *I do not even begin to think of unity when the Trinity bathes me in its splendour. I do not even begin to think of the Trinity when unity grasps me.*

St Gregory of Nazianzus

WHEN WE HAVE EXERCISED our priesthood at Mass by offering all we have tried to do for God since we last took part in the Sacred Mysteries, He always returns our generosity with love without measure. It is His other-worldly love that draws us ever more deeply into the very life of Christ as He is now, risen and glorified. However the ultimate meaning of this 'Holy Communion' can only be fully appreciated by realising that it leads us, not just to share in the life of 'The Risen Christ', but into His very action, into His pure and perfect love of His Father.

In other words we are drawn up into the infinite vortex of life and love that endlessly reaches out from the Son and into the Father and from the Father into the Son. It is into this Trinity of everlasting life and love that Jesus came to invite us. This is the home for which we were created and for which we yearn the more we experience 'the love that surpasses all understanding' reaching out to embrace us. However this profound giving and receiving that is the heart and soul of the sacred mysteries will soon degenerate into a dry and barren formalism unless what is celebrated there is practised again and again each day of our lives. The morning offering can be one of the most effective reminders to consecrate each moment of each day to the relentless giving and receiving that enables us to be drawn ever more deeply into the life of the Three in One.

However when we have offered up the forthcoming day we need to pause for a few moments further to pray for the profound union that only God can give to those who open themselves to receive Him. This love will not only bring us to 'at-one-ment' with Him but with our true self, that is otherwise broken and fragmented and separated by selfishness from those around us.

"Father, we pray that we may come to know and experience the Holy Spiritual love that endlessly revolves between you and your Son so that we may be at one with you, with ourselves, and with those You wish to love through us. Amen."

11 Interior stillness

Silentio (silence)

As vocal prayer is interiorised and purified it goes beyond itself into the prayer of silence which characterises the state of union with God.

Pére Louis Bouyer

SO FAR WE'VE BEEN DOING all the talking. Now it's time to be silent, to rap ourselves in deep interior stillness, so that we can become docile and sensitive to the action of God as He penetrates us more and more fully. In short we need time in our daily prayer to do what we should do immediately after receiving Holy Communion. Now the longer we can remain still and open to God's action in this 'Spiritual Communion' the more we will enable Him to fill us with the self-same love with which he filled Christ.

At first this is the most difficult thing to do in prayer, as it is in all relationships. In any relationship there tends to be a certain insecurity at first and we tend to talk too much to cover our embarrassment. It usually takes a long time getting to know someone before we can simply be together in a mutual silence that somehow seals the friendship. When everything has been said that needs to be said the greatest joy is simply to be together in a silence that transcends even the most potent words. After all what do words do but unite those who are separate from each other, but in the perfect one there is a perfect and blissful silence.

This is the high point in any relationship and it's exactly the same in our relationship with God. Prayer always begins by using many words or prayers, but it always ends up in a profound silence when we begin to experience the love of the One to whom we have been speaking, sometimes to shattering degrees of intensity. Although it may be difficult to begin with, therefore, it is essential that we try to cultivate this inner silence so that we may eventually come to experience something of the fullness of love for which we were born.

Knowledge alone does not change a person permanently for the better, but love does. That's why the saint who was once a self-centred sinner like the rest of us becomes the sort of other-considering person whom we all admire and wish to emulate. Silence is ultimately the spiritual womb where even the worst of us can be re-conceived by the same Spirit who conceived Christ in the first place.

12   Prayer and petition

Intercessio (intercession)

Prayer is the raising of one's mind and heart to God or the requesting of good things from Him.

St John Damascene

MOST OF OUR ACTIONS are limited by the world of space and time in which we live, but prayer isn't, it takes us into another dimension where the laws of space and time no longer apply. That other dimension is Christ who is not only the alpha and the omega, the beginning and the end of all space and time, but present in every moment of it to everyone simultaneously. When prayer raises us up out of our world and into His it enables us to be united with all who are in Him, whether they lived in the past, the present or will live in the future.

That's why there is no such thing as private prayer in the Christian tradition, even though the person praying may be totally alone in their own home, in the local church or in the furthest reaches of the most distant desert. They are united with all those who are in the family of Christ, with Mary and Magdalene, with Peter and Paul, with Benedict and Bernard, Francis and Ignatius, Catherine and Teresa. This is why the sincere prayer of the least of us is powerful far beyond our own personal spiritual resources alone.

All my immediate family are dead now but I try to remember them each day. I try to pray for others too who have asked me to pray for them and whom I might otherwise forget despite the promise I made at the time. There's a wider world too that needs our prayers, but rarely asks for them. The daily newspaper and even the news on the television can be used as an aid to prayer. When we hear about those whose suffering makes us feel so helpless, remember them at the time we set aside for daily prayer. Now just as you can't give to every good cause, you can't pray for every good cause by name either, so it's often a good thing to adopt one or two causes that have a special meaning for you.

Although praying for others may seem to be the poor cousin of other spiritual exercises that appear more attractive, it's certainly not the case. In praying for others we not only forget ourselves but also open ourselves to receive, for it is in giving that we receive without even realising it.

13 Preparing for action
Actio (action)

Whenever you do it to the least of my brothers then you do it to me.

Matthew 25:40

WHEN WE HAVE FINISHED PRAYING for others we can pray for ourselves and ask God to give us the grace to *act* in the most Christ-like way possible in the forthcoming day. This is the time to try and anticipate all the jobs we have to do and the people we have to meet so that we can try to meet them as Christ would have done, and serve them as He did.

It's a good opportunity to make a few resolutions too, to do humdrum tasks as well as we can, like clearing our desks, doing the shopping, or preparing the meals and the other jobs that can help transform our day when they are done with love. There are more important things that we could also resolve to do that are all too easy to keep putting off. There's always that friend or relative who's sick or in need whom we should 'phone, or write to, or even visit for a few minutes. We may need to make a resolution to apologise to one of the family, a friend or someone at work for the way we behaved towards them the previous day.

Sometimes there are very difficult decisions that we have to make that can cost us dearly, like standing up for someone who's been abused by authority at work or elsewhere. We may have to make a decision to speak the truth when no one wants to hear it, or to stand up for what we know is right at great personal cost.

Once we have seen what we ought to do and decided to do it we must refuse to listen to that soothing little voice inside us that will inevitably try to lead us astray. It will appeal to the procrastinator, the sluggard and the coward that's in us all to renege on the resolutions we'd made a short time before.

One of the most important truths of the spiritual life, that we neglect at our peril is that we won't ultimately be judged by the wonderful feelings we've experienced in prayer. We won't be asked how many ecstasies we've had or even how many miracles we've worked or people we've healed, but how we've served God in the neighbour in need.

14   Perfect love

You'll never love someone unless you know them, but you'll never really know them unless you love them.

William of St Thierry

FRANCISCANS HAVE TRADITIONALLY taught us to pray by emphasising how we should use our hearts, while Dominicans stress the use of the mind. Which is right? Both of them are right! That's why the great Benedictine writer, William of St Thierry, said that you'd never love someone unless you know them, but you'll never really know them unless you love them.

The trouble is when I first decided to start taking prayer seriously I'd just fallen in love for the first time and I simply couldn't conceive loving God with my whole heart and mind and with my whole being, as I had come to love my girl-friend. Compared with her God seemed so abstract, so distant, so far away. "That's precisely why God became man, so that we could love him in Jesus," my parish priest explained to me.

The trouble was I had difficulty with the idea of loving another man even if He was the Son of God, at least not as I'd recently come to understand the word. It might do for girls but it wouldn't do for me. Then I came across a book that seemed to resolve my difficulties. It explained how in the

Old Testament God was sometimes called a Mother as well as a Father and was endowed with feminine as well as male characteristics. It showed how some of the Fathers of the Church spoke of what they called the *anima* and the *animus* in God.

In other words God is neither male nor female, but the qualities of maleness and femaleness can be found uniquely balanced and brought to perfection in Him and perfectly expressed in His love for all that He created. These same qualities must therefore be found in Jesus Christ in whom the fullness of the Father's love is to be found here on earth. That's why in responding to His love, men and women can respond equally, if differently and both ultimately find their completion in Him.

Thanks to that book what I'd originally thought impossible suddenly became possible and the ambiguity about trying to love Jesus no longer held me back. I decided to study Him more and more deeply so that I could come to love Him and in loving Him come to experience the only love that could change me permanently for the better.

15 Lectio Divina

To be ignorant of the scriptures is to be ignorant of Christ.

St Jerome

HOW DOES ANYONE SPEAK to anyone else? There's nothing mysterious about human communication. We get to know someone by listening to the words they use. The spaces between people are bridged by words. They enable us to find out more about them, to draw closer and closer to them. This is why Christians have always regarded the Bible with awe from the earliest times, because it contains the words that bridge the gap between God and man – God's words. It even goes a step further by showing how God's words were eventually embodied in the flesh and blood of Jesus Christ. When we learn to listen to His words we learn to listen to God. When we learn to love Him we learn to love God.

Despite the time given to silence in the 'memory-jog' for prayer, we've still been doing most of the talking. However for prayer to lead on to generate the quality of love that will alone permanently change us for the better, we must learn to listen.

This is why all authentic Christian prayer begins not by flinging oneself into obscure states of transcendental awareness, but by trying to listen to God's words, most particularly as embodied in the words of Jesus Christ. When we read the scriptures then, slowly and prayerfully allowing them to sink into our hearts, we listen to the word of God speaking to us now. This is how the early Christians used to pray in a method of prayer that was called *Lectio Divina* or the divine or sacred reading. It was so called, not just because they believed the words they read were inspired, but because they believed that they too would be inspired as they read them, by the same Holy Spirit who inspired them in the first place. They believed that through the holy readings they would be led on and into a sort of profound conversation with God that would lead them on and into what St Paul called "the height and depth, the length and breadth of God's love that surpasses the understanding".

This is why whatever other methods of prayer we may at times find helpful, we must never forget and always turn back to the Bible as the Christian prayer book 'par excellence'.

16 Prayerful reading
Lectio (Read)

Reading supplies material for the understanding of truth, meditation prepares the material, prayer elevates it, and contemplation rejoices in it.

Hugh of St Victor

FOUR LATIN WORDS HAVE traditionally been used to describe how *Lectio Divina* can lead serious-minded Christians onward to experience the Love that surpasses all understanding. The words are *Lectio* (Read), *Meditatio* (Reflect), *Oratio* (React), and *Contemplatio* (Repose).

The early Christians knew no other method of meditation. Many of them knew whole passages, if not all of the Gospels off by heart. They had no other prayer book to hand, nor did they have need of them. When the Desert Fathers used the scriptures, most particularly the New Testament and the Psalms, they were not interested in how much they read, but in how deeply they penetrated the sacred texts. They would read a few verses at a time, going over them for a second and a third time, poring over them, entering more profoundly into their dynamic inner meaning.

Then they would pause in moments of deep interior stillness to allow the same Spirit who inspired the scriptures in the first place, to inspire them also. When they had savoured one particular text they would reverently move on to another and repeat the process, leaving pauses for silence, for the impact of the words to seep into the very marrow of their being. As this prayer grew more and more intense, the moments of silence would become more and more prolonged until in the end words would give way to periods of profound inner contemplation.

Learning to read the scriptures (*Lectio*) means learning to read in a new way and learning to listen too as we've never really listened before. You see we are so bombarded with reading materials from all sides every day of our lives, that we have had to acquire a habit of reading at a breathtaking pace of knots. Every day there are the newspapers to be read, mountains of junk mail to sift through, memoranda to be absorbed and letters and bills to be dealt with. Our only concern is to glean the relevant facts as quickly as we can and to move on to something else. If we apply the same techniques to the way we read the scriptures it won't enable us to get to know Christ more deeply. They should be read as we would read good poetry, endlessly going over them to plunder their contents.

This is the beginning of true *Lectio Divina*.

17   Meditation

Meditatio   (Reflection)

*You should show yourself diligent, indeed
constant, in the reading of scripture, until
continual meditation fills your heart and
forms you, as it were, after its likeness.*

John Cassian

HAVING READ AND RE-READ the sacred texts it's time to reflect
(*Meditatio*). Pore over them again and again, ruminate on
them, as St Augustine would say, allow the inner meaning of
every word to seep deep down into the very marrow of your
being so that their dynamic impact can register with effect.

Now in order to facilitate the use of this profound meditation
some people find it helpful to recreate the scene in which the
sacred words were first spoken in their imaginations. Let's
suppose that you've chosen to meditate on those profound
words of Jesus at the Last Supper. Begin by setting the scene
in your imagination. Picture the Apostles preparing the
tables, see Christ coming into the room, watch the way he
moves, look into his face when he speaks, then mull over his
every word, trying to penetrate their inner meaning.

The same sort of scene-setting could be used to build up the
atmosphere before meditating on other Gospel texts. The
Passion of Christ, for instance, would lend itself to this

method of praying. Don't just think of what Christ went through in your mind, go back in your imagination and place yourself in the event. You are amongst the soldiers at the scourging, one of the crowd during the carrying of the cross, an onlooker at the actual Crucifixion. You see everything as it happens, you open your ears and hear what is said and then you open your mouth and begin to pray. Although this approach does not appeal to everybody, no one should be put off just because it could lead to an emotional response.

We are not dealing with pious fantasy here but with the most momentous historical events in human history. The word was made flesh precisely so that people of flesh and blood could understand and see God's love made tangible. Christ's death was a brutal and painful reality through which the Word, who was made flesh, speaks of love in a way that is intelligible to all.

To neglect the Passion as a primary source of Christian meditation and prayer is to neglect the most important manifestation of God's love that ever took place. "We are not blocks, we are not stones, we are not senseless things". If we cannot eventually respond in kind to such love then there is something wrong with us.

18   Heartfelt prayer
Oratio (Reaction)

If the heart does not pray then the tongue labours in vain.

St Bernadine of Siena

THE MORE WE PENETRATE the inner meaning of the sacred texts the more we feel moved to react prayerfully with our hearts to what we have assimilated (*Oratio*). Real prayer begins now as we start trying to raise our hearts and minds to God, as we respond to the inspired words upon which we have been reflecting.

To start with the truths of the faith are too big, too enormous, almost too incredible for us to take in effectively. When I first heard that the stars in the nearest galaxy, Andromeda, were two million light years away I simply could not take it in. The distances were too enormous for my mind to cope with. It's exactly the same with the truths of our faith, at least to begin with. They are too much for us to cope with, too great for us to take in, it's as if our minds are paralysed by their transcendent enormity. We simply cannot penetrate or comprehend their meaning.

It's the same with our emotions too, they can only respond to a stimulus of a certain degree of intensity. When I first heard of my mother's death I didn't react, it was all too much for my emotions to cope with. It's the same with the truths of the faith, at least to begin with. However with good will and, with genuine and that means continuous effort come what may, things will gradually begin to change for the better.

This state of mental paralysis gradually begins to lift. The slow meditation on the sacred texts suddenly begins to bear fruit, the spiritual understanding begins to stir and the emotions are touched and begin to react. What began as rather dry academic knowledge about God changes and begins to strike with an ever-deepening impact. Knowledge begins to turn into love, as the love that God has for us begins to register with effect. Nobody can remain the same when they realise that another loves them. We respond automatically, the emotions are released and we begin to express our love and thanks in return. This is the beginning of real prayer that will grow with depth and intensity as the truth of God's love is brought home time and time again in so many different ways through slowly poring over, digesting and assimilating the sacred texts.

19 The beginning of contemplation

Contemplatio (Contemplation)

Contemplate and share the fruits of contemplation with others.

St Thomas Aquinas

AS THE IMPACT OF THE GOSPEL message begins to explode with maximum effect, the believer finds that even the most extravagant words do not sufficiently voice the depth of feeling that they experience welling up from within. In the end the words of thanks, praise, adoration and love give way to silence that says far more than the most potent man-made means of expression. The slow meditative penetration of the texts now opens out and envelops the whole person as the believer is ever more deeply absorbed into a silent contemplative gaze upon God. The most powerful and poignant expressions of the new relationship with God seem to be emptied of their meaning in face of the reality. All one wants to do is to remain silent and still in the simple loving gaze upon God that has traditionally been called *contemplation*.

It is the fruit of this profound prayer that is, in the eyes of St Thomas, the perfect preparation for sharing the faith with others. He could have said that we should first meditate and then share the fruits of our meditation with others or pray and share the fruits of prayer with others, but something even more profound is required. We must persevere for long enough in prayer to experience for ourselves something of the love that we are called to share with others in sublime mystical contemplation or we will have little to give. In this contemplation in which the whole person, heart and mind, body and soul is more united than ever before, a subtle change begins to take place. Initially it was through meditating on God's love, as embodied in the human body of Jesus, that had led the believer to contemplation, but now a change gradually begins to take place. Meditating on God's love as it was embodied in the historical Christ gives way to contemplating His love as it is now, pouring out of the risen Christ, whether the believer realises this or not at the time. The first was generated with God's grace and human endeavour, the second is a pure gift of God.

However, before the gift of contemplation can lead to the full union for which the believer now craves, a purification begins to take place so that the selfish seeker can receive the Selfless Giver without any let or hindrance.

20   Glorified love

As the Risen Christ is a true man and the same man that He was, both in body as well as in soul before the resurrection, so He has still the same human affections now.

Thomas Goodwin

THE WHOLE POINT OF AUTHENTIC CHRISTIAN meditation is not just to come to know and love the most divine and loveable of human beings who once walked on this earth, but to love Him as He is now. Nevertheless, at first sight it may seem that we who have not known Him face to face are at a disadvantage. Although that cannot be denied, we are nonetheless advantaged in a unique way too, that was denied to those who shared in His friendship whilst He was still on earth.

In entering into human weakness Christ was inevitably limited by having a human body that could only be at one place at a time. Getting to know Him therefore involved coming and going, meeting and departing. Not even His closest disciples could be with Him all the time. However, after the resurrection all that changed. Now, raised outside the limitations of space and time He could be with everyone at one and the same time, and furthermore He could be with them all the time, because He could be with them from the inside through love.

Now the resurrection did not mean that He became transformed into some sort of disembodied spirit quite other than the man who walked the highways and byways of Palestine, as He was at pains to make clear. That's why He showed the marks of his suffering to His disciples, made those who doubted touch Him and shared food with them. If He wasn't exactly the same person as before it wasn't because He was less of, but more of a man, because His glorification meant that all His human qualities were brought to perfection. They were refined, distilled, and transformed by the Holy Spirit, who raised Him from the dead, into a supernatural love through which He could be available to all.

Now this is the love that gradually begins to enter into the believer most effectively through contemplation. Through a single shaft of love all the human perfections that were originally embodied in His human body whilst He was on earth are transmitted to the believer. Now He can continue His work on earth through as many as are prepared to receive Him and with as much of His love and compassion as they allow Him to embody in them.

21   Food for prayer

It is not only the scriptures, but anything inspired by them, that can inspire us with the prayer that leads to contemplative union.

Francisco de Osuna

IN ORDER TO USE *Lectio Divina* most effectively it's perhaps best to turn to the Gospels to begin with, most particularly the Gospel of St. John. Turn to his famous discourses, especially his profound spiritual discourse at the Last Supper, from chapter 13 to chapter 17. There's enough food for prayer there for a lifetime. Then turn to the other Gospels, the letters of St John and St Paul, the Acts of the Apostles and then to the other New Testament writers.

However the method used in *Lectio Divina* can be used to explore other religious texts as well. Use them to meditate more systematically and more deeply on your favourite spiritual poems and hymns. There are many profound and beautiful hymns that we only glance at briefly every now and then when we sing them in church. Hymns like 'Lead Kindly Light', or "Come Holy Spirit' etc. The Hymnal can be a rich source of material for meditative prayer. Some of the modern folk hymns are ideal too. The music may be of varying quality, but the words are often both scriptural and profound.

Meditate in the same way on some of the liturgical texts like great Eucharistic prayers for instance. We rarely have time to penetrate their profundity when they are being read for us at Mass. One of the advantages of using these prayers in this way is that it helps to remind us that our prayer is continually moulding us into Christ's own prayer. There are many other liturgical prayers and hymns that can be used for personal prayer in this way. The 'Gloria' is a perfect example and so are many other ancient poems, hymns and sequences used throughout the liturgical seasons, helping to site our personal prayer into the context of each successive liturgical season. Use the psalms too, especially those that you feel speak to you in a special way in your particular needs. These were one of the main sources of spiritual nourishment for the Desert Fathers.

The use of liturgical texts in this way helps to build a bridge between public and personal prayer. Too often they are seen as two entirely different and separable departments of Christian prayer, when they should be seen and experienced as two indispensable ways of entering into the prayer of Christ.

22   Traditional devotions

Anything that helps to raise the heart to God is Prayer.

St Francis de Sales

SADLY THE ANCIENT AND TRADITIONAL way of leading ordinary Christians onwards through meditation to contemplation through the scriptures was lost sight of for a series of reasons that are happily no longer relevant today. You see, when Christianity spread along the famous roads built by the Romans it found itself in rather rude and primitive surroundings compared with the sophisticated empire into which it was born. How could you give the scriptures to people who could not read or write? From the earliest times it had always been the custom to translate the Liturgy and the Scriptures into the language of the people. However, how could you do this when the people had no language, or at least no written language sufficiently developed to allow such a translation to take place?

By the time this became possible and more and more people were able to read, it was reformers unacceptable to the traditional Church who first gave the people the Word of God in their own language. This is why the Church has for many centuries frowned upon, if not positively discouraged the reading of the scriptures. During these centuries when ordinary people were starved of the scriptures, it was the prerogative of the great saints and spiritual leaders to present the central mysteries of the faith to the people in a way that could lead them to prayer. Simple devotions grew up for the illiterate, techniques of mental prayer were introduced and methods of prayer came into vogue, culminating in the meditation manuals that we have known almost up to the present day.

Many of these helps to prayer have stood the test of time, like the Rosary, the Stations of the Cross, Devotions to the Sacred Heart, the Exercises of St Ignatius for example, and others. In general these various improvisations were good because they genuinely re-presented the authentic teaching and spirit of the Gospels. In so far as they continue to do this they can still be used with profit and help guide people to genuine sanctity, as they have done so often in the past. However, the scriptures have been opened to all once again, so they ought to be put in pride of place as the means of guiding any serious searcher through meditation to the profound contemplative union with the One who inspired the sacred scriptures in the first place.

23 The Rosary

It is an incomparable prayer, the lay person's breviary, that can lead onwards to the heights of sanctity.

Leo XIII

THERE IS ONE TRADITIONAL FORM of prayer that embraces almost every other and can be taught to children before they can read and write. For centuries it has guided the faithful from the foothills of the spiritual life to the heights without them ever realising that they were going anywhere. That's why you rarely find arrogance or pride in someone whose spiritual ascent has been made thanks to the Rosary.

A person may begin by just saying each individual prayer slowly and prayerfully, trying to grasp their meaning and then making them their own. Then in time they learn how to recite them in such a way that the usual distractions are sedated so that they can meditate on each individual mystery in turn. Gradually meditation turns into a profound loving contemplation as the most loveable human being the world has ever known, is seen doing the most human things in the world with such love, and being hated to death for it. When this happens the beads no longer need to be counted nor do the prayers need to be said as a few heartfelt words rise from within to express feelings that begin to overflow for the One whose love seems to surpass all understanding.

Then, when words give way to moments of joyous contemplative stillness, there is no need to do anything but savour in silence the fullness that has been received and experienced. When these moments pass and distractions re-appear, it's time to return to counting the beads again and concentrating on each successive prayer or to meditating on the mysteries once more. When moments of darkness come and dryness and aridity seem to make all else impossible it's time to turn to another form of prayer traditionally called *The Prayer of the Heart*. It is designed to keep the heart's deepest desire fixed on God, when the feelings and emotions that once helped them seem to do nothing but generate distractions. The prayer that is now counted on the beads may be simply "Thy will be done", "Jesus Mercy, Mary help" or just "Jesus" or some other such prayer that expresses a person's deepest need "when the well runs dry".

This is how so many of our parents and grandparents were taught to pray and then led on into mystical prayer by the Holy Spirit without them even realising it.

24   The Sacred Heart

In the New Testament the heart is the seat of the divine action which transforms the Christian.

John L. McKenzie

AMONG THE LAST WORDS OF JESUS in St John's Gospel were "Blessed are they who have not seen and yet learnt to believe". Throughout the subsequent centuries Christian art has tried to help those of us "who have not seen" to come to know and love not just the Christ who lived in history but the Christ who still lives in Majesty. As memories grew dimmer Christian art became more and more important, particularly for those who were illiterate. The representations of Christ that dominated the first Basilicas were of Christ in Majesty, the 'Pantocrator', the ruler of all. This tended to make Christ appear as rather distant until, in the wake of the crusades, the Holy Land was opened up to the west and a new spirituality began to flourish, thanks to St Bernard and St Francis, that emphasised the humanity of Christ again. Their influence can be seen in painters like Giotto and in the great artists of the renaissance. However, thanks to St Margaret Mary, a new popular art began to represent not just Christ as He was, but as He is now, with a glorified body bursting with uncreated love. The Sacred Heart is the same as the Pantocrator, but now He does not appear as distant, for He rules with all the human love that filled Jesus whilst he was on earth, but transformed by what became of Him in heaven.

If devotion to the Sacred Heart has at times been trivialised by bad taste in the cult surrounding it or the art used to promote it, it should never be forgotten that it proclaims a profound truth that is the central truth of our faith. Jesus is not dead, He has risen and is alive now bursting with uncreated life and love that pours out of His heart relentlessly and into the hearts of all who would receive Him. For two centuries this devotion counteracted 'Catholic Calvinism' or Jansenism with its narrow-minded kill-joy moralism, by proclaiming the love of the Risen Christ in a way that even the simplest could understand. No one should allow their artistic sensibilities to prevent them from appreciating this profound truth that was revealed in a unique way to St Margaret Mary. The Sacred Heart is not just incarnate love but incarnate loving, who will transform all who open their hearts to receive Him.

25   *Pray as you can, not as you can't*

Dom John Chapman

DESPITE EVERYTHING THAT HAS been said and the various suggestions that have been made, none of them may be of any help. That doesn't matter. What does matter is that you use whatever method of prayer that helps you best. Ways, methods or techniques of prayer are only means to an end. They are in fact no more than props to help keep our hearts and minds raised and open to God. They are means to this end and should be used as such. There are no perfect means, just different means for different people at different stages of their spiritual journey.

What helps a person at the outset of their journey may not help them as they get into their stride. What helped them when they were going downhill with the wind at their back might be of little use when they are struggling uphill with the wind in their face. What helped them in the spring might not help them in the autumn of their life.

No matter what is said in this little book, or elsewhere for that matter, "Pray as you can, not as you can't". Whatever method of prayer helps you here and now to keep "raising your heart and mind to God" whilst at the same time keeping distractions at bay, is an ideal method of prayer for you.

Now be sure that you will never find any man-made method of prayer that will completely destroy the distractions that pester us at the best of times. In fact you can't really pray without them. You see, if you ever find that they have completely disappeared then you will either have fallen asleep or been transported into an ecstasy! If you have fallen asleep you're not praying because you are doing nothing, and if you are having an ecstasy you're not really praying either because God is doing everything. The place where our praying is done is between the sleep and the ecstasy where we continually practise repenting as we repeatedly try to turn back to God despite the distractions that try to make us turn elsewhere.

Prayer is the place where selfless giving that is the heart and soul of all prayer is practised until, under the influence of the divine, human loving is brought to perfection. Whatever means of prayer helps you to do this is good even if it doesn't help anyone else.

26   The essence of all prayer

Prayer is trying to raise the heart and mind to God.

Cardinal Basil Hume

WHATEVER METHODS OF PRAYER we might find helpful they will get us nowhere if there is something fundamentally wrong with our attitude. Let me explain what I mean.

Two main attitudes have dominated the approach to God in prayer throughout the history of Christian spirituality. Before the renaissance the older religious orders emphasised the action of God while the newer orders, founded after the rise of humanism, tended to emphasise the action of man. Both are orthodox, but both have in-built dangers that have often led people into spiritual cul-de-sacs.

Those who put all the emphasis on what God does can easily forget what they should be doing to co-operate with Him, and they fall into Quietism. This leads to a sort of presumption as they present themselves to God in prayer like suet puddings waiting to be soaked in syrup! On the other hand, those who stress the importance of what we can do, can forget what God does and can easily fall into what used to be called Pelagianism. They act as if everything depended on them. It can lead to a sort of spiritual pride, to an arrogance of heart and mind that destroys the prayer that they seem to believe depends more on their endeavour than on God's.

In order to avoid the danger of presumption Cardinal Hume introduced the word *trying* into the traditional definition of prayer. In order to avoid the danger of falling into pride I would like to introduce the word, *gently* to stress that our endeavour will get us nowhere without God's help. If we get angry or upset at our failure it's not because we've failed God, but because we've failed ourselves and the goal we thought we could attain by our own endeavour.

Prayer then is *gently trying* to raise the heart and mind to God. Despite having a perfect definition of prayer most of us will spend much of our lives trying to walk the spiritual tightrope between pride and presumption, continually falling off once this side then the other. Then in God's time not ours the Holy Spirit will eventually reward the person of good will who perseveres despite their human failures. They will finally receive the perfect balance that enables them to keep their hearts and minds open to God, free of the pride or presumption that can prevent them receiving the love that they long for more than anything else.

27   Pray at all times

*We have not been commanded to work,
to keep watch and to fast constantly,
but it has been laid down that we are to
pray without ceasing.*

Evagrius Ponticus

SINCE EARLIEST TIMES serious-minded Christians have tried to find a way of observing the Gospel precept to pray at all times. The Desert Fathers tried to observe it by taking a sentence or phrase from the scriptures, that struck them during the recitation of the divine office, or a short prayer of their own choosing that somehow summed up their deepest personal need. Then they would continually call it to mind and use it throughout the following day. Although the prayer may be conceived in the mind it must be drawn down into the heart from where it will rise to God.

Now by the heart they understood not primarily the emotions and feelings, but, as in the scriptures, the moral and spiritual centre of the whole person. So *prayer of the heart* means the prayer of the united person, prayer in which the one who prays is totally identified with the prayer. Abbot Isaac said, "When you rise from your bed let this prayer send you to your knees and thence send you forth to your work or business, and let it follow you about all day." It may be a prayer like, "Lord to the rescue", as suggested by Abbot

Macarius or, "O God, come to my aid, O Lord, make haste to help me", suggested by Abbot Isaac. This was a prayer that St Benedict found so helpful that he insisted that his monks should recite it before each hour of the divine office. The simple prayer, "Jesus help" or simply, "Jesus" developed into the *Jesus prayer* – "Jesus, Son of God, have mercy on me, a sinner". That is perhaps the best known *prayer of the heart* that has been used to the present day.

St Augustine was first to call these prayers ejaculations, whilst later spiritual writers called them aspirations. In more recent centuries such aspirations as, "Jesus mercy, Mary help" or, "Sacred Heart of Jesus I put my trust in Thee', often originated from popular devotion. When used properly they still embody all the characteristics of the *prayer of the heart*. Whatever we call these short prayers they can still help a person to aspire to the *prayer without ceasing* by helping to sanctify each day, making it a continual offering to God.

28   The prayer without ceasing

He prays without ceasing who unites prayer to works and good works to prayer. Only in this way can we realise the precept to pray without ceasing.

Origen

JOHN THE BAPTIST CALLED PEOPLE to repent or turn to God because His kingdom was coming. Jesus called people to repent because the kingdom was close at hand, but St Peter called people to repent because the kingdom had come. The very moment when Jesus was glorified was the very moment when the fullness of life that filled Him began to overflow onto and into all who would repent or turn and open themselves to receive it. We can only hope to achieve the *prayer without ceasing* when we begin to realise that every moment is a time for repentance, for turning to receive the love of God that continually surges out of the Risen Christ.

Repentance is practised inside of prayer by using whatever means of prayer helps to do this, despite the distractions that do not prevent but actually facilitate repentance. However, outside of prayer repentance can still be practised each time a person tries to turn to God in the neighbour in need and by offering to God everything we do, even the most humdrum tasks by doing them with care and integrity. In this way every moment of every day can become a time to turn to God no matter whether we are trying to pray or trying to live out our vocation in the world. Now it is in giving, or in repenting inside of prayer, that we receive the love that enables us to keep turning to God outside of prayer. Here repentance continues, if we keep trying to turn to Him in the neighbour in need and in the way we try to offer all and everything we do, uniting our sufferings to the sufferings of Christ.

Notice how many times the word *try* or *trying* has been used. We do not achieve the *prayer without ceasing* when we have managed to turn to God without any let or hindrance, because nobody can ever achieve that permanently. The most we can ever do is to try our best. It is by trying our best to turn to God at all times that we attain the *prayer without ceasing*. That's why Simone Weil said, "a person is no more than the quality of their endeavour". This is how God will ultimately judge us all – not by what we think we have achieved or failed to achieve but by the quality of our endeavour, by how best we have tried.

29 True humility

When you stop falling you are in heaven, but when you stop getting up you are in hell!

Peter Calvay

ONLY OUR LADY WAS conceived without sin, that means that the rest of us weren't. That's why we are continually falling both inside and outside of prayer, whether we like it or not, and that includes the saints too. Now the difference between them and us is not that they didn't fall and we do, but that they learnt how to use their inevitable failures to their advantage. St Paul was the first to pen what is in fact the great secret of the spiritual life. It is simply this – that God's power works most perfectly in human weakness, gradually transforming it. That's why no one can progress in the spiritual life without the humility to know their weakness and their need of the only One who can help them.

What further distinguishes us from the saints is the speed with which they turned for help. We keep procrastinating because pride prevents us from accepting our failures and so valuable time is wasted. In fact the greater the pride the greater the length of time it takes before a person finally gets enough humility to seek the forgiveness that they need and the grace to begin again. Like St Peter the saints immediately turned back to God the very moment they realised they'd failed Him. They did this repeatedly without the endless delays that stymie the spiritual growth of the rest of us.

Whether in or out of prayer the measure of spiritual advancement can always be determined by the speed with which we turn back to God from the distractions, the temptations, or the sins that try to turn us away from Him. However, what all the saints discovered was that this speed could only be maintained with the help and strength from God. That's why though they may have differed from one another in everything else, they were one in their daily commitment to prayer. They knew, without a shadow of a doubt, that without it they had no power to do anything of any real value or worth, let alone advance in the spiritual life. That's why each of them in different ways all echoed the words of St Teresa of Avila when she said, "There is only one way to perfection and that is to pray and if any one points in another direction they are deceiving you."

30 The impossible made possible

With love you may bring your heart to do whatsoever you may please. The hardest things become easy and pleasant, but without love you will find anything not only difficult but also impossible.

John of Bonilla

LIKE MOST EUROPEAN CATHOLICS I was born and brought up in the aftermath of the Renaissance, influenced by a spirituality that owed as much to the rise of humanism as to the Gospel of Christ. Naturally I thought that if I were to attain the sanctity to which I aspired it would be primarily the result of my own effort. I was in effect a Christian stoic, a Pelagian who had failed so comprehensively to make myself into the saint of my dreams that I was about to give up the spiritual life for good.

It was then that I came across 'Pax Animae' written by the Spanish Franciscan John of Bonilla in 1588. It was a spiritual gem untouched by the spirit of humanism. Reading it was the nearest I had come to a Damascus road experience. It immediately enabled me to see that I had been misled into believing that I could be the architect of my own perfection. Its very first paragraph, from which I have quoted, showed me why I had failed and what I ought to do to succeed. The rigorous asceticism that I had adopted to make myself perfect had done nothing but exhaust me. Now I could see that I would achieve nothing without coming to know and experience the self-same love that animated the man I wanted to emulate more than any other. I needed a new type of asceticism that would not dissipate my energies trying to do the impossible, but which would enable me to do the "one thing necessary".

In short I needed to gather what little resources I had to create quality space and time in my daily life for the profound prayer that would give me access to the same love that filled Jesus Christ and inspired everything that he said and did. I knew that this love would have to be experienced if it was going to give me the inner security that would alone do for me in some small measure what it had done in full measure for Christ. I had a new asceticism with which to substitute the old and I called it 'the asceticism of the heart and mind'.

31 Child-like simplicity

Unless you become as a little child you cannot enter the Kingdom of God.

Jesus Christ (Matthew 18:3)

THE SPIRITUAL LIFE SEEMS to have become so complicated over the years that you almost feel you need a couple of degrees in theology just to understand it before you can even attempt to live it! Yet it is essentially simple, so simple that you need the simplicity of a little child to see it. You see, there is only one thing that is necessary and that is love. Not our love of God, but His love of us.

In other words, Christianity is firstly a mysticism not a moralism. It's not primarily concerned with detailing the perfect moral behaviour that we see embodied in Christ's life and then trying to copy it virtue by virtue – that's stoicism, not Christianity, and it's doomed to failure. It is primarily concerned with teaching us how to turn and open ourselves to receive the same Holy Spirit who filled Him. The more we are filled with His love then the easier it is to return it in kind, as the divine suffuses and then strengthens human love so that it can reach up to God and out to others. Then, and only then are we able to love God with our whole hearts and minds and with our whole being and to love our neighbour as ourselves.

The trouble is we make the same mistake with Christ as we do with the saints. We read their lives backwards. We read about their rigorous lives, their superhuman sacrifices and their heroic virtue, and believe that the only way we can be like them is to do likewise. If we only read their lives forward instead of backwards then we'd see that they were only capable of doing the seemingly impossible because they first received the power to do it in prayer.

If we try to be and do what they did without first receiving what they received then our brave attempts will inevitably end in disaster. True imitation of Christ or any of His saints means first copying the way they did all in their power to receive the Holy Spirit who inspired them. That's essentially all we have to do. That's why the spiritual life is so simple, if only we had the simplicity of a little child to see it.

32 | Asceticism for all

First seek God and His Kingdom and
everything else will be given unto you.

Jesus Christ (Matthew 6:33)

THE ASCETICISM FOR THE BEGINNER then is quite simple – don't give up anything you like or enjoy except when it prevents you from giving quality space and time to God in prayer each day. If you think it's too easy then try it and stick to it and you'll soon find it's not quite so easy as you thought. So don't let first enthusiasm fool you into heroics that you will never sustain. Now when you have persevered for long enough you will gradually begin to receive and then experience the love that will enable you to do what is quite impossible without it.

When a person falls in love and begins to experience being loved, then there is nothing that they wouldn't do nor any sacrifice that they wouldn't make for their lover. In fact they positively look for things to do, the harder and the more exacting the better, to enable them to show the real quality of their love. What was impossible to a self-centred egotist only a short time before becomes not only easy but also their greatest pleasure.

It is exactly the same in the spiritual life. The exemplary behaviour, the extraordinary self-discipline and the heroic sacrifices made by a person who begins to experience the love of God are not the results of an arrogant stoic trying to make themselves perfect. They are the actions of someone desperate to express their love in behaviour that could not be maintained for long without the love that sustains it. All the little pleasures and pastimes that were thought indispensable before suddenly become dispensable, and with the greatest of ease. Virtues that were noticeable by their absence before are born of the love that envelops them!

You see, when the love of God strikes a human heart it strikes it as a simple ray of light strikes a prism. Just as that light is then diffused and transformed into all the colours of the spectrum, so the love of God is diffused and transformed into all the virtues and gifts that are needed as the believer seeks to acquire them. In short, first seek God and His Kingdom which is love, and everything else you want or desire will be given to you.

33 The sacrament of the present moment

The present moment is always full of infinite treasures, it contains far more than you have the capacity to hold.

De Caussade

WHENEVER YOU WATCH ANY SPORT at the highest level you cannot but be impressed with the dedication of the participants. It's the quality of their single-mindedness that draws the attention. The moment they begin their preparation it's as if they enter into a time-free zone where they are able to put everything out of their minds in such a way that they can live and act fully in the present. If they allow anything from the past to disrupt their concentration, it's instantly dismissed. Nor must anything from the future disturb them either. Just a few moments' indulgence imagining themselves receiving their trophy, or celebrating with their friends could mean losing their prize.

It should be exactly the same with preparation for prayer. We need some sort of countdown to help us drop out from the hectic life that is so often forced upon us, to prepare to turn on and tune in to God. Just as different athletes find their own rituals we need to find our own. It may simply be lying down for a rest, reading some spiritual or inspiring book, exercising, going for a swim, listening to music, practising yoga or whatever helps to relax us. This is all part and parcel of the asceticism of the heart and mind that is going to help us enter into that time-free zone when we begin to pray. It is here that we can first begin to enter as fully as we can into the present moment, by ridding ourselves of anything from the past or the future that can draw the attention away from fixing our gaze fully upon God. This is the only place on earth where time can touch eternity.

In order to sanctify this place and consecrate it to God the early monks first practised private confession so that no past guilt would disturb them. They even confessed the temptations that might induce them to desecrate holy ground by inducing them to live in the future. God cannot be encountered in the past or in the future but only, as de Cassaude saw so clearly, in what he called "the sacrament of the present moment". This is the only moment when time touches eternity, and prayer is the offering that makes it a holy place, where the human and the divine first meet and mingle before being united.

34 From meditation to contemplation

He doesn't know what's the matter, all at once God has retired to a distance. It is absolutely impossible to move the heart. He remains cold, frozen.

Pére Gabriel de Ste Marie-Madeleine

THESE ARE JUST SOME OF THE WORDS used to describe the typical experience of a young person whose initial success in prayer seems to come to a sudden and inexplicable halt. Their dismay is accentuated because after months of daily meditation, knowledge had led them on and into a heartfelt love of Christ that they'd never experienced before.

This inevitable turning point in the spiritual journey is not a sign of failure but of success. Success in using all the inner resources to raise the heart to God has enabled Him to accept the believer's offering and has begun to draw their love towards His own. However all they experience is an unfulfilled desire for God that pursues them in and outside of prayer. It makes them seek out solitude where they seem to find nothing save a thousand and one distractions that prevent the pure and unimpeded contemplation of God that is their deepest desire. The memory, the imagination and the understanding that once helped them raise their hearts to

God now seem hell-bent on dragging it down to earth again. The reason for this is simple. The heart's attention is so fixed in what is called *obscure contemplation*, that it is no longer free to control the inner resources that it had used a short time ago to rest in God with a sweetness that has totally disappeared.

Once a spaceship comes under the gravitational pull of the planet, the canisters of fuel that thrust it through the earth's atmosphere must be jettisoned. In the same way, once first fervour has led the believer to experience the mysterious pull of God's love, the prayer forms that helped them before must now be jettisoned. Any attempt to return to the prayer of first fervour will not only prove fruitless but also impede the new form of prayer, which will lead them onward and into *The Mystic Way*. The high point of prayer in 'first fervour' is sometimes called *Acquired Contemplation*, because it is partially self-generated, unlike *Mystical Contemplation* to which the believer is now called, which is a pure gift of God.

35 The mystic way

A naked intention directed to God and Himself alone is wholly sufficient.

The Cloud of Unknowing

AT THE BEGINNING OF *The Mystic Way* the author of *The Cloud of Unknowing* says that, it seems as if there is a "Cloud of Unknowing" between you and God. Now in order to keep your "naked intent" fixed upon Him to enable your heart's desire to pierce through the cloud, you must take a short prayer or a single word and repeat it gently over and over again.

The prayer will help keep your heart fixed on God whilst at the same time helping to stem all the distractions by smothering them, as it were, under a "cloud of forgetfulness". The words suggested by the author of the "Cloud of Unknowing" are *God* or *Love*, because that's what you desire more than anything else in this strange new world, or the word *Sin*, because this is what you want to flee from more than anything else. Now whether these words are used or some other short prayer, it is imperative that you continue to give exactly the same time to prayer that you gave before.

It was easy to pray when prayer seemed easy and was so full of peace and joy. However in the spiritual life, as in the married life, real love is shown when you are prepared to go on giving when you seem to be in an emotional limbo-land and when you seem to be receiving nothing in return. This is exactly how a person feels at the beginning of the mystic way and that's why it is the place when real selfless loving is learnt as never before. The bounty-hunters who have only been praying for what they could get out of God won't last very long, they will soon cut and run and begin to seek elsewhere what they can no longer find in prayer.

St John of the Cross said that ninety per cent give up prayer at this point – because they don't understand what's happening and there doesn't seem to be anyone else who does. What is needed now is a good spiritual director who knows by personal experience how to guide them forward. Meanwhile read *The Cloud of Unknowing* or *The Dark Night of the Soul* written by St John of the Cross to help people at this crucial point in the spiritual journey.

36   The prayer of the heart

*I cried to God with my whole heart, which
is with my body and soul and spirit.*

St John Climacus

LET ME SUM UP THE PRACTICAL TEACHING on the use of the
prayer of the heart in contemplative prayer, since the time of
the Desert Fathers. Instead of choosing a single word to
begin with, use a full sentence. Choose one that somehow
sums up how you feel at the time, how you are relating to
God who seems to have taken His leave of you. Sentences
from the scriptures for instance could be used like, "My God,
my God why have you forsaken me?" or, "Father, that this
chalice might be taken away from me, but your will be done,"
or "Out of the depth I cried to you, O Lord, Lord hear my
prayer." Sometimes a sentence from the hymnal would seem
appropriate like, "Lead, kindly light amid the encircling
gloom", or turn to the Jesus Prayer designed specifically for
this particular moment in the mystic way, "Jesus, Son of God,
have mercy on me, a sinner".

Don't try to dwell on these prayers or intellectually inspect
them, they are not to help you meditate, but to contemplate
or to gaze upon God with a simple uncluttered heart and
mind. When you choose a sentence, choose one that seems
to sum up exactly how you feel, not how you think you ought
to feel. Then repeat it over and over again to help keep your

attention fixed on God although He seems to have disappeared behind a cloud of unknowing. In time you'll find the full sentence too long and you'll feel the need to reduce it to, "My God, my God" or "Out of the depth" or "Lead, kindly light" or "Have mercy on me, a sinner". Then the time will come when a single word is all you feel inclined to use like "God" or "Jesus", or some other word like "mercy" or "help" that you feel best represents your needs in this strange dark night.

Finally no words are necessary, they have only been a device to help a person keep turning to gaze upon God. Then, under the magnetic pull of His love, words become less and less necessary to say what is said more profoundly in silence. When this happens in mystical prayer the presence of God progressively fills the silence, drawing the believer up into ever more awesome experiences of His all-enveloping love.

37 Purifying love

The Dark Night is an inflow of God into the soul purging it of its habitual ignorances and imperfections.

St John of the Cross

IN MEDITATION IT IS JESUS CHRIST who is the object of prayer but at the beginning of the mystic way, it is always God. The believer begins to wonder where the Sacred Humanity has gone. It has gone nowhere, it is we who have gone more deeply into the Sacred Humanity where, in Christ, with Him and through Him, we are praying and offering our sufferings with His, to the Father.

Now our prayer is more powerful than ever before even though we may not feel that we are praying at all. The person who remains faithful in this prayer becomes ever more open to receive the inflow of God's Holy Spirit who begins a profound purification. This enables us to be more at one with Christ in His act of loving the Father than we have been in the past, and more open to receive from the Father the Love that draws us relentlessly onwards into the life of the three in one.

You see, unlike things cannot unite, the selfish cannot be united to the selfless. That's why we have to be purified so that we can be united with God and come to experience the fullness of Love that we desire more than anything else.

The beginning of the mystic way then is not full of sweetness and light, but of bitterness and darkness, because we are not yet purified enough to experience His presence, but only the presence of the sinfulness and selfishness that keeps Him at bay. That's why so many people pack up prayer at this stage, wrongly believing that they are on the wrong path.

Now at this particular point in the journey a person not only sees their sinfulness as never before, but also their utter helplessness to do anything about it. The experience is not meant to turn a person away from God, but to turn them to Him, as the only One who can help them. However this purification takes some time, months or even years, depending on commitment to prayer, before they can begin to experience the presence of the Holy Spirit preparing them for union with God.

38 Waiting on God

Waiting alone in the semi-darkness for God to do whatever He pleases sums up what it means to follow Christ.

Sr Wendy Beckett

ST CATHERINE OF SIENA said that if you haven't any patience at all, it's ten to one you haven't got any other virtues either that are worth writing home about. She insists that true patience can only be found through prayer. Now she doesn't just mean praying for patience, though that's a good start, but practising patience inside of prayer itself. Most of us give up prayer before we've really started because nothing happens, and we are too impatient to learn how to wait on God.

No matter where you begin or how you progress, the time will come when you have done all that you can do, and then you have to learn how to wait on God. It is here that a person learns by practical experience that it is not they who are in control, but God. He comes when he chooses, not when we choose. Our job is to be ready at all times to receive Him.

Waiting on God is easy when he seems to be close at hand listening to all we have to say and granting any request that we make of Him. That's what's called cupboard love. But the real test of love is when we are prepared to go on loving, go on giving, go on waiting when he seems far away, when He doesn't seem to be listening at all, or granting what is asked of Him. St John of the Cross makes it quite clear that anyone who perseveres in prayer will inevitably come to the place where one has to wait on God in darkness amidst dryness and aridity. Here there will be not only many distractions but temptations too, against faith, hope and charity.

When there's no experience of the presence of God for prolonged periods of time you begin to ask, not just where is God, but is there a God, and if there is no God, what hope is there? Only the person who is prepared to persevere waiting on God despite these temptations will be purified and refined in such a way that they are ready and prepared to receive the One who comes when you least expect Him. Then His love will gradually transform them into the One they have chosen to follow.

39   Experiencing being loved

You can do more in a month with contemplation than in a lifetime without it.

Père Lallement

IN ORDER TO GROW TO FULL STATURE a human being not only needs to see and accept their weaknesses, but to experience the love that will enable them to become the person they aspire to be. That's why, when a person has persevered long enough in the 'Night' to show they are more interested in God than in what they can get out of Him they are at last open to receive the love that they need. The experience of this love is so delicate to begin with that a person is only aware that they would be spiritually diminished without the prayer that seems so full of dryness and aridity. Then in what St Teresa of Avila calls the *prayer of recollection* a gentle absorption in God brings a sense of inner peace despite the distractions.

This same experience increases as the awareness of God's action rises in intensity to what she calls the *prayer of quiet*. Then when the intensity increases to the point where there are no longer any distractions to hinder absorption in God she calls it the prayer of *full union*. This is ultimately surpassed when the intensity of God's love cannot be sustained and moments of oblivion or *ecstasy* occur. These experiences of divine love have a profound effect on the receiver who is never quite the same again. It not only affects them personally but others too, who see something of the One whose love they are receiving at work within them. These brief but awesome experiences are but the prelude to a far more permanent experience that doesn't just take place in the head, but envelops the whole person, body and soul. This is sometimes called *divinisation* or *theosis* in the Eastern Church. In the west it has been called the *transforming union* or the *mystical marriage*.

Now marriage is not the end of love but a new beginning that should deepen and deepen, in this case to eternity. In this, the ultimate experience of God's love on earth the whole person, heart and mind, body and soul, tangibly feels something of the love that draws them into the vortex of life and love that endlessly revolves between the Father and the Son. This experience gradually becomes permanent. At last the *prayer without ceasing* becomes attainable as the believer continually experiences the joy of being caught up in the Mutual Love that endlessly flows between the Father and the Son. It almost feels as if the life of the Three in One opens to admit a fourth!

40 The only way to perfection

Without Me you have no power to do anything.

Jesus Christ

IN HIS FIRST LETTER St John makes it quite clear that the first principle of the spiritual life is love, but lest we misunderstand him he says, I don't mean our love of God but God's love of us. You see, the truth of the matter is we can't possibly love God unless He gives us the power to do it. That's why the first question that is asked by all the great spiritual writers from the beginning is not how do we love God, but what do we have to do to receive His love.

Love cannot be forced. Forced love is a contradiction in terms. Although God is 'Loving', that is His very nature and He is loving us all the time, that love will remain totally ineffective, not in Himself, but in ourselves if we do not freely choose to receive it. Prayer is simply the word used to describe the way in which we set about creating the quality space and time in which to turn to receive that love so that we demonstrate what we believe, not just by what we say but by what we do.

Then, and only then, as God's love begins to enter into the person who chooses to receive it, will that love enable them to return His love in kind. Then and only then will that same person be able to start loving others, for the Gospel makes it quite clear that "without Me you will have no power to do anything".

We might be brimming over with ideas and ideals for humanity, but something further is required if we are going to be more than armchair idealists. It's all very well to talk about caring for the deprived and neglected, stamping out racial and colour prejudice, welcoming the refugee and bringing peace and harmony to those who reject them, but it's all 'pie in the sky' unless our hearts are changed from within. God's love is the only power that can permanently change not just our minds and our hearts, but the way we act, for the world that Christ wants to continue serving through us.

That's why I want to end as I began by quoting St Teresa of Avila – "There is only one way to perfection and that is to pray, if anyone points in another direction then they are deceiving you."

Appendix

GETTING STARTED

Prayer to be real must arise from the desire to love and be loved, to become vessels of the Holy Spirit for the suffering world about us.

Sr Wendy Beckett

Morning Prayer

Whilst seeking a pattern of prayer in your own words you might like to try this, based on the text that you have just read. It starts with the words with which St Benedict first taught his monks to begin the divine office, and includes eight prayers based on the memory jog – Parousia –

O God, come to my aid
O Lord, make haste to help me.
Glory be to the Father and to the Son and to the
Holy Spirit. Amen.

O God, you are my God, for you I long;
For you my soul is thirsting.
My body pines for you
like dry weary land without water. (Psalm 62)

A Profession of Faith

O God, I know and believe that You are all loving, that Your love is perpetually poised to possess me. Penetrate and possess me now, permeate my whole being as I try to turn and remain open to receive You. Melt my heart of stone, re-make it, and re-mould it, so that it can at all times be open to receive You. "For unless You enthral me I shall never be free, nor ever chaste except You ravish me".

A Prayer of Adoration

I adore you with my whole being as you possess my being with your inexhaustible and unfathomable fullness. May my total prostration before You enable me to plunge with ever greater penetration into You as You penetrate me. Give me the grace to praise, honour and thank You, as much as I am able and more than I am able, not just in words, but in a life that I now consecrate to You.

A Prayer for Reconciliation

Father, forgive the sins that have hardened my heart against You in the past and help me to overcome them in the future. I am truly sorry for them and with Your grace will never let my pride delay me from turning back to You the moment I fall. Make me ever more sensitive to all that separates me from You and from those I wish to love as You love me.

A Prayer of Offering

Lord, for tomorrow and its needs I do not pray, help me to offer myself to You just for today. Through everything I say and do, through every joy and sorrow, through every pleasure and pain I suffer, I offer this day to You. I know You will receive it for no merits of mine, but for those of Jesus Christ, in whose own offering it is made.

A Prayer for Union

Father, You always give without measure, give me now the love that You gave to Jesus that I may be taken up into His risen life. In Him I pray that I may be drawn more deeply into the love that endlessly revolves between You and Him. I only dare to make this prayer because Jesus first made it for me and has made it possible through the Spirit He has sent into my hearts.

A Prayer for Spiritual Silence

Father, You know well enough that our hearts are restless "till they rest in You". Let my heart rest in You now as You begin to make Your home in me and I begin to make mine in You. Help me remain still and silent for a few moments to relish what I have received *(Pause for a few moments silence)*. Give me the grace to experience Your love more and more deeply, to receive the inner security I need to become what You want to make of me.

(In order to maintain attention on God in the pause for silence a short prayer could be repeated gently whenever distractions threaten to draw the attention elsewhere.

*A prayer such as 'Come, Lord,' or 'Come, Lord Jesus' would
be ideal or some other short prayer of your choosing).*

A Prayer of Intercession

Lord, I pray for my parents, my family and my friends,
particularly for those who have died or who are sick, and
especially for those who have asked me to pray for them.

I pray too for those people whom I have heard about in the
news, who are in need, particularly for those suffering for
what they believe to be right or for the faith that we can too
easily take for granted. Lastly I pray for myself and for my
needs, but most of all for my greatest need, for the deep
inner security and peace that only Your love can bring.
Please hear all these my prayers and petitions, not through
my own merits, because I haven't any, but in and through
Your Son Jesus Christ and all who are alive in His love. Amen.

*NB. It's important to name the people for whom you pray
individually whenever possible.*

A Prayer for Christian Action

Lord, as I now go through the details of the day ahead with
You, inspire me with the wisdom that I need to live it as I
should. Fill me with the same Spirit that inspired Jesus so
that I may be inspired too in everything I say and do. If I
can't love everyone as I should, help me to do them no harm
and give me the sympathy and compassion of the Person in
whose footsteps I want to walk.

*Now say one: "Our Father", one "Hail Mary" and one
"Glory Be".*

Evening Prayer

O God, come to my aid
O Lord, make haste to help me.
Glory be to the Father and to the son and to the
Holy Spirit. Amen.

O God, you are my God, for you I long;
For you my soul is thirsting.
My body pines for you
like dry weary land without water. (Psalm 62)

A Profession of Faith

Lord, I know You have been with me throughout this day, though my work has often kept You at bay. Make me always work in future with honesty and integrity and with such care and compassion for others that You can be with me in everything that I do. Then I know you'll always be with me, living in me, working through me and giving to others what I can never give without You.

A Prayer of Adoration

Lord, never let the intimacy that You have chosen to share with me make me forget how You utterly transcend me in every way. Though You are infinitely distant You are infinitely near, for you inhabit the inner marrow of my being, where I now humbly adore You. Thank You for being with me and for all You have given me today, for life itself and all and everyone that has made it worth living.

A Prayer for Reconciliation

Lord, although no day goes by without me failing You, You never fail me. Show me how I have kept You at bay, as I now try to review my life this day and ask forgiveness yet again for what prevents You possessing me as You would wish. (*A short pause to review our behaviour in the past day.*) I am deeply sorry for failing You yet again. With your grace I will try better next time and try to be quicker in turning for the forgiveness that You will never refuse me.

A Prayer of Offering

Lord, accept the offering that I have made of this day with all its joys and sorrows. Accept all the matchwood crosses that I have tried to bear, because they're offered through the cross that Jesus bore for me. Now I offer up my sleep, make it deep, make it re-invigorate me to dedicate another day to serving You.

A Prayer for Union

I know that it is in giving that we receive, so may my giving help me receive Your love a little more fully with each passing day. Enable me to experience something of that love in the home You promised to make deep down within us. Then enwombed in Your love, I will at last experience the security that I need to grow into my true self in Jesus Christ in whom You want us all "to live and move and have our being".

A Prayer for Spiritual Silence   S

Lord, help me to put aside everything that has fragmented me throughout this day, if only for a few moments. Teach me how to be still and come to know that You are my God, not just with my head, but with every feeling in every fibre of my being. Then, let me experience something of "the peace that surpasses the understanding" to draw me together again in You and in Jesus Christ Our Lord. Amen.

(Once again, in order to maintain attention on God, as you pause for silence, a short prayer could be repeated gently whenever distractions threaten to draw the attention elsewhere. A prayer such as 'Come Lord' or 'Come, Lord Jesus' would be ideal or some other short prayer of your choosing)

A Prayer of Intercession   I

Lord, as I pray for my family by name help me to picture them in my imagination, so that my prayer can be more personal and directed to their individual needs. *(Pause to visualise those for whom you now wish to pray and ask God to help them in your own words)*. Let me pray for my friends too and for those who have particularly annoyed me during the day. Finally Lord, help those poor, deprived and suffering people, whom I have heard about in the news today. You have given me so much, help me always to remember them in my prayers and to do what I can for them whenever the opportunity arises.

A Prayer for Christian Action

Lord, I will be good for nothing tomorrow unless You help me to get a good night's rest. Whilst I am asleep act within me to revitalise my mind and body. When I wake up fill me with the spiritual and physical vigour that I need to offer another day to You and try to live it, as I should, in and through Jesus Christ Your Son Our Lord.

Now say one "Our Father", one "Hail Mary" and one "Glory Be".

❊ ❊ ❊

A Suggestion – taken from an ancient tradition traced back to the Desert Fathers

When you're already in bed take a short prayer and repeat it slowly and prayerfully. It might simply be the word 'Jesus', or the full Jesus prayer – 'Jesus, Son of God, have mercy on me, a sinner'.

This prayer and others like it came to be used, most particularly in the Eastern Church, with slow rhythmical breathing. It was not just a device for relaxation, but for reminding the believer of the all-pervading action of the Holy Spirit. You see, the ancient Jews believed that a person's breath was their life-principle, their spirit, so naturally they believed that God's breath was His life-principle, His Spirit. As a mark of respect, God's breath or His Spirit came to be called the Holy Spirit. So deep rhythmical breathing that often accompanied short prayers 'of the heart', helped remind them of the ever incoming Spirit who dwelt within them with ever increasing power the more they prayed.

It can be a reminder to us too, particularly when preparing for sleep. The prayer 'Come, Holy Spirit' for instance, can accompany the slow intake of breath followed by the prayer 'conceive Christ in me' as we breathe out. With the next breath pray again 'Come,

Holy Spirit' followed by 'fill every part of me', and again with the next breath 'Come, Holy Spirit', followed by 'bring Christ to birth in me'. Then the three prayers could be repeated again and again. Other short prayers could be used like 'Come, Lord', or 'Come, Lord Jesus'· or whatever short prayer you feel helps you best. When this practice becomes a habit it can be far more effective than the sleeping pills that many turn to today and there are no side effects either!

Whenever you have finished trying to pray be at peace. You have done the best you can, now leave the rest to God remembering the words of Padre Pio –

"Pray, trust and don't worry"

❊ ❊ ❊

Post Script

All the themes in this book are detailed at greater length in David Torkington's *Trilogy on Prayer – The Hermit, The Prophet, The Mystic* (Mercier Press, Cork. Distributed by McCrimmon Publishing Co. Ltd. - 01702-218956, Email: mccrimmons@dial.pipex.com) and *Inner Life* and *A New Beginning* (Darton, Longman & Todd 020 8875 0155.) In his most recent book *Dear Susanna* (Darton, Longman & Todd) he shows the historical reasons why personal prayer has been so neglected in recent years and why the 'Christian renaissance' that is long overdue cannot be brought about without it. David has also produced two tapes that can be obtained from Alba House New York, *Praying made Simple* and *Loving made Simple*.

Web page: http://www.davidtorkington.com